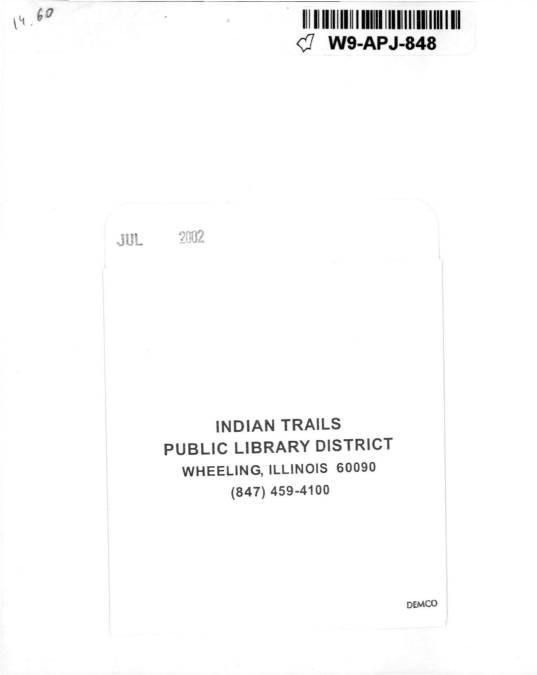

14.60

W9-APJ-848

What Are
Levers?

by Helen Frost

Consulting Editor: Gail Saunders-Smith, Ph.D.

Consultant: Philip W. Hammer, Ph.D.
Assistant Director of Education
American Institute of Physics

Pebble Books

an imprint of Capstone Press
Mankato, Minnesota

Pebble Books are published by Capstone Press
151 Good Counsel Drive, P.O. Box 669, Mankato, Minnesota 56002
http://www.capstone-press.com

1 2 3 4 5 6 06 05 04 03 02 01

Library of Congress Cataloging-in-Publication Data
Frost, Helen, 1949–
    What are levers? / by Helen Frost.
    p. cm.—(Looking at simple machines)
    Includes bibliographical references (p. 23) and index.
    ISBN 0-7368-0846-9
    1. Levers—Juvenile literature. [1. Levers.] I.Title. II. Series.
TJ147 .F77 2001
621.8′11—dc21
                                                              00-009867

Summary: Simple text and photographs present levers and their function as a
simple machine.

Note to Parents and Teachers

The Looking at Simple Machines series supports national science
standards for units on understanding work, force, and tools. This
book describes levers and illustrates how they make work easier.
The photographs support early readers in understanding the
text. This book also introduces early readers to subject-specific
vocabulary words, which are defined in the Words to Know section.
Early readers may need assistance to read some words and to use
the Table of Contents, Words to Know, Read More, Internet Sites,
and Index/Word List sections of the book.

Table of Contents

A lever is
a simple machine.

bar

A seesaw is a lever.
A lever has a bar
that moves.

fulcrum

A lever also has a fulcrum that stays in place.

Force is put on one part of a lever.

load

force

12

Another part of the lever
lifts the load.

A lever makes
lifting easier.

load

force

fulcrum

A wheelbarrow is a lever.

fulcrum

force

load

18

A broom is a lever.

load

force

fulcrum

A fishing pole is a lever.

Words to Know

broom—a large brush with a long handle; it is a third-class lever because the force is applied between the load and the fulcrum.

force—a push or pull on an object; force makes objects start moving, speed up, change direction, or stop moving.

fulcrum—the point on which a lever rests or balances; a lever creates the most force when the fulcrum is close to the load.

lever—a bar balanced on a fulcrum; a lever changes a small force into a larger force.

seesaw—a long board balanced on a support in the middle; it is a first-class lever because the fulcrum is between the force and the load.

simple machine—a tool that makes work easier; work is using a force to move an object across a distance.

wheelbarrow—a small cart with one wheel at the front; it is a second-class lever because the load is between the force and the fulcrum.

Read More

Armentrout, Patricia. *The Lever.* Simple Devices. Vero Beach, Fla.: Rourke, 1997.

Rush, Caroline. *Levers.* Simple Science. Austin, Texas: Raintree Steck-Vaughn, 1997.

Welsbacher, Anne. *Levers.* Understanding Simple Machines. Mankato, Minn.: Bridgestone Books, 2001.

Internet Sites

The Lever, a Basic Machine
http://www.robinsonresearch.com/
TECHNOL/the_lever.htm

Levers
http://www.brainpop.com/tech/simplemachines/
lever/index.weml

Levers
http://www.eecs.umich.edu/mathscience/
funexperiments/agesubject/lessons/beakman/lever.html

What Is a Lever?
http://www.professorbeaker.com/lever_fact.html

Index/Word List

Word Count: 66
Early-Intervention Level: 9

Editorial Credits
Martha E. H. Rustad, editor; Kia Bielke, cover designer and illustrator; Kimberly Danger, photo researcher

Photo Credits
Capstone Press/CG Book Printers, cover
David F. Clobes, 6, 8, 10, 12, 16
Photo Network/Myrleen Cate, 18
Photri-Microstock/Tom McCarthy, 20
Visuals Unlimited/Mark E. Gibson, 1; Jeff J.Daly, 14

The author thanks the children's section staff at the Allen County Public Library in Fort Wayne, Indiana, for research assistance. The author also thanks Josué Njock Libii, Ph.D, Associate Professor of Mechanical Engineering at Indiana University–Purdue University.

24